THE ROYAL NAVY IN FOCUS 1950-59

M106

EDITOR'S NOTES

During the fifties the number of ships in the Royal Navy steadily declined. By the end of the decade the last battleship was in Reserve, never again to see service; only four aircraft carriers were operational with another three in Dockyard hands; just four cruisers were in commission with two more completing. What a change the fleet had seen in a decade.

The "old style" of warfare—ship against ship, gun against gun—was gone. The emphasis had changed with air and underwater warfare predominating. The increased speed of aircraft and submarines had led to the need for faster, more complex, and hence more expensive vessels—that took longer to build—to combat them. The large numbers of wartime-built frigates and escort destroyers became obsolescent and were laid up, scrapped or relegated to training or policing tasks in distant waters. A large number of other destroyers, however, being faster, were converted to anti-submarine frigates with greatly enhanced detection equipment and weaponry.

Experiments with surface-to-air missiles began in earnest with the conversion of GIRDLE NESS to a Guided Weapons Trials Ship and gas turbine propulsion started to be seen at sea in GREY GOOSE. Substantial programmes of new construction were undertaken with new classes of frigates, submarines, minesweepers, fast patrol boats and seaward defence boats being added to the fleet to replace outdated tonnage and to fill operational requirements highlighted by the Korean War.

As in the two previous titles in this series we have carefully selected (from the large portfolio of photographs of this era held by Wright & Logan) what we hope will represent most of the ship types active during this decade.

Mike Critchley
Liskeard
Cornwall

HMS ADAMANT (October 57)

Submarine depot ship built by Harland & Wolff at Belfast and launched 30.11.40. Completed in 1942 and served in the Eastern Fleet until late 1944 and then serviced her flotilla in Australian waters. 6.50 Flagship of Senior Officer, Reserve Fleet, Portsmouth. 10.54 commissioned as parent ship to the 3rd Submarine Squadron based on Rothesay until early 1964 when she became parent ship to the 2nd Submarine Squadron at Devonport. Listed for disposal 3.66 and arrived Inverkeithing 9.70 to be broken up.

HMS ALAUNIA (June 53)

Former Cunard liner built by John Browns at Clydebank and launched 7.2.25. Requisitioned as an armed merchant cruiser and commissioned 27.9.39. Served in the Halifax Escort Force. 1944 converted to a Repair Ship and served in the East Indies. 1949-56 used as static training ship for engine-room ratings at Devonport although she was present at the Coronation Review at Spithead 6.53. 10.9.57 arrived at Blyth to be broken up.

HMS ALBION (June 57)

Centaur class light fleet carrier built by Swan Hunter on the Tyne launched 6.5.47 and completed 1954. 11.56 took part in the Suez campaign and served, until 1960, in the Far East and Southern Oceans. 1.61-7.62 converted to Commando Carrier at Portsmouth and after trials left (3.11.62) for the Far East. Involved in the Malayan and Indonesian border dispute of 1963. 1967 assisted during the withdrawal from Aden. Her final commission took her to the Arctic and the Far East before being laid up 1972. 10.73 sold to commercial interests for use in the North Sea oilfields but conversion plans were dropped and she arrived at Faslane 11.73 to be broken up.

HMS ALDERNEY (July 50)

'A' class submarine built by Vickers-Armstrongs at Barrow; launched 25.6.45 and completed 10.12.45. Subsequently refitted with Snort and half-shield to gun (see photo). In the mid-fifties was modernised at Portsmouth to give greater underwater speed and more silent operation. Paid off for disposal 2.68. Broken up at Cairnryan 1972.

RFA AMHERST (July 59)

Built at Glasgow in 1936 as a passenger/cargo liner for the Furness Line and named FORT AMHERST. 12.51 purchased by the Admiralty for use as a Naval Armament Carrier and renamed AMHERST, entering service (after modifications) in 7.52. Operated by the Royal Fleet Auxiliary Service, principally between the UK and the Mediterranean. Laid up at Plymouth 7.62. 1963 sold and broken up.

HMS APOLLO (June 53)

Fast minelayer built by Hawthorn Leslie on the Tyne; launched 5.4.43 and completed 12.2.44. Her first task was to lay 1170 mines south west of Seine Bay in 4-5.44 to protect the Normandy beach-head. 7.6.44 ran aground off Normandy. After repairs laid mines to counter U-boat activity in UK coastal waters. 22.6.45 left the UK for the Pacific returning one year later and paying off into Reserve at Sheerness. 1951 recommissioned for Home Fleet service and served as Despatch Vessel until 1961, frequently flying the flag of the C-in-C. Visited Leningrad 10.55. Paid off 4.61. 28.11.62 arrived at Blyth to be broken up.

HMS ARK ROYAL (1955)

Built by Cammell Laird at Birkenhead over a period of nearly 12 years. Launched 3.5.50 and completed 25.2.55. The largest aircraft carrier to have served in the Royal Navy. Served in all theatres during her career which was interspersed with lengthy periods of inactivity under refit or reconstruction. 4.12.78 Her last deployment ended at Devonport. She was de-equipped and on 22.9.80 left under tow for breaking up at Cairnryan.

HMS ARTEMIS (May 59)

'A' class submarine built by Scotts at Greenock launched 26.8.46 and completed 15.8.47. 1949 refitted with Snort and gun removed. 15.6.53 Coronation Review at Spithead. 1957 began modernisation at Portsmouth, emerging in 1959 with a changed silhouette (compare with ALDERNEY). 1.7.71 sank alongside her berth at Fort Blockhouse. 6.7.71 raised. 2.72 listed for disposal and later the same year sold to H G Pounds, Portsmouth to be broken up. 1978 demolition commenced.

HMS ARMADA (September 58)

Battle class destroyer built by Hawthorn Leslie at Hebburn-on-Tyne. Launched 9.12.43 and completed 2.7.45. Joined 19th Destroyer Flotilla in the British Pacific Fleet until 1947 then returned to the UK and paid off into Reserve. 7.49 recommissioned for 3rd Destroyer Flotilla in the Mediterranean. 5.1.53 sailed from Malta for Chatham, and paid off. 8.56 recommissioned for 3rd Destroyer Squadron in the Mediterranean. Returned to Portsmouth 19.12.56 and served with the Home Fleet until 5.60 when she paid off for disposal. 12.65 towed from Chatham to Inverkeithing, to be broken up.

HMS BADMINTON (July 55)

Coastal minesweeper built by Camper & Nicholson at Gosport; launched 14.10.54 and completed 5.7.55. Served in the 108th Minesweeping Squadron in the Mediterranean. Subsequently returned to Home Waters and joined the VERNON Squadron, serving as leader of the squadron from 7.64 to 1.65. 3.68 listed for disposal. 24.4.70 sold to be broken up.

HMS BARFOSS (July 58)

Bar class boom defence vessel built by Simons at Renfrew and launched 17.2.42. Operated from Portsmouth in the mid-fifties and later used as a civilian manned degaussing rangelaying vessel. Sold out of service and broken up in Belgium July 1968.

HMS BECKFORD (July 57)

Seaward defence boat launched 27.4.55. 12.64 became seagoing tender for the Mersey Division of the Royal Naval Reserve and subsequently renamed DEE. Chartered 1968 by the Plessey Group of Companies and renamed ROBERT CLIVE. 1.69 returned to the Mersey Division RNR and reverted to DEE. 1982 disposal list at Devonport. 1984 sold to Pounds Marine Shipping Ltd.

HMS BERMUDA (July 59)

Built by John Brown on the Clyde, launched 11.9.41 and completed 21.8.42. Commissioned for service in 10th CS Home Fleet. 11.42 covered North African landings. Mid-1943 operated in the Bay of Biscay. From 8.44 to 4.45 refitted for service with British Pacific Fleet. 19.6.47 returned to the UK. 1951-52 Flagship of C-in-C South Atlantic. 1953-54 in 1st CS Mediterranean. 1955 Home Fleet. 11.55 to 10.57 refit on the Tyne. 1957-62 Home/Mediterranean commission. 1963 laid up. 26.8.65 arrived at Briton Ferry to be broken up.

HMS BELFAST (July 59)

Improved Southampton class cruiser built by Harland & Wolff at Belfast. Launched 17.3.38 and completed 3.8.39. She was the largest cruiser in the Royal Navy of the fifties. 11.39 severely damaged by mine in the Firth of Forth. After a three year rebuild she spent the rest of the war in home waters, taking part in the sinking of the German battlecruiser SCHARNHORST and in the invasion of Normandy. Served in the Far East 1945-47, 1948-52 (including action in the Korean War) and 1959-62. 1956-59 reconstructed at Devonport. 1963-71 Reserve at Devonport and Portsmouth. From October 1971 has been berthed in the Pool of London as a museum ship.

HMS BIRMINGHAM (June 52)

Southampton class cruiser built at Devonport Dockyard. Launched 1.9.36 and completed 18.11.37. 16.11.37 commissioned as Flagship of 5th CS, China Station. From 1940 served in the Home Fleet, South Atlantic, Eastern Fleet and Mediterranean until being damaged by torpedo in the Mediterranean 28.11.43. Repairs lasted until 1.45 then served in Home and East Indies waters. 1950-52 reconstructed at Portsmouth Dockyard then joined the 5th CS in the Far East, serving in the later stages of the Korean War. 1956-59 Home and Mediterranean Fleet. 2.9.60 left Devonport under tow to be broken up at Inverkeithing.

RFA BLACK RANGER (May 59)

Built by Harland & Wolff at Govan launched 22.8.40. Operated throughout the war in the Home Fleet based at Scapa and served as escort oiler on a number of convoys to North Russia. Post-war was principally based at Portland as Training Oiler, frequently accompanying the Home Fleet on cruises and exercises. The submarine HMS THULE surfaced under her in the English Channel 18.11.60 and sustained some damage. 7.73 sold for mercantile service and renamed PETROLA XIV.

HMS BOLD PIONEER (March 57)

Fast patrol boat built by White at Cowes launched 18.8.51 and completed 1.53. Could be fitted as torpedo boat or gunboat. Attached to HMS HORNET Trials Squadron and shown fitted with a 3.3 inch gun forward. Sold out of service 22.10.58.

HMY BRITANNIA (May 54)

Royal Yacht built by J Brown at Clydebank launched 16.4.53 and completed 14.1.54. Her maiden voyage was to the Mediterranean, sailing from Portsmouth 14.4.54 escorted by the frigate LOCH ALVIE. Other voyages during the fifties took her to Sweden, Canada (twice), Denmark and the Mediterranean again. Her home mooring is off Whale Island in Portsmouth Harbour. Still in service (1985).

HMS BROADSWORD (October 51)

Weapon class destroyer built by Yarrows at Scotstoun, launched 5.2.46 and completed 4.10.48. Joined the 6th Destroyer Flotilla, Home Fleet. Served in Home waters until paid off into Reserve in 1953. 1957-58 converted to fleet radar picket at Rosyth and commissioned 30.9.58 for the 7th Destroyer Squadron on Home/Mediterranean service until 1.63. Reduced to Reserve and (11.63) listed for disposal at Portsmouth. 1965 de-equipped. 25.4.68 towed from Portsmouth to Rosyth to be tested to destruction by the Naval Constructional Research Establishment. 8.10.68 the hulk arrived at Inverkeithing to be broken up.

HMS BROCKLESBY (October 57)

Hunt class destroyer built by Cammell Laird at Birkenhead launched 30.9.40 and completed 9.4.41. Fought with distinction in Home and Mediterranean waters during the war, earning the battle honours of English Channel 1942-43, Dieppe 1942, Sicily 1943, Salerno 1943, Atlantic 1943, Adriatic 1944. 1945-47 aircraft target ship. 1947-51 Reserve at Portsmouth. 1952 joined 2nd Frigate Squadron for service as Asdic Training and Trials Ship for the Admiralty Underwater Weapons Establishment at Portland. 22.6.63 paid off at Portsmouth. 28.10.68 arrived Faslane to be broken up.

RFA BULLFINCH (January 57)

Cable ship built by Swan Hunter on the Tyne and launched 19.8.40. 15.6.53 Coronation Review at Spithead. Classed as a Royal Fleet Auxiliary and then as a Royal Maritime Auxiliary Service ship before being laid up for disposal at Plymouth 8.8.75. Broken up at Blyth, arriving there 14.2.80.

HMS BULWARK (June 57)

Aircraft carrier built by Harland & Wolff at Belfast launched 22.6.48 and completed 4.11.54. 1956 took part in the Suez Canal operations. 1959-60 converted at Portsmouth into a Commando Carrier and served almost exclusively East of Suez throughout the sixties except for periods under refit in the UK. In 1972 acted as Headquarters Ship for the withdrawal of the British Armed Forces from Malta. Although relegated to Reserve in 1976 she was brought forward again in 1977 because of delays to her replacement—HMS INVINCIBLE. 27.3.81 arrived at Portsmouth to pay off. 16.4.84 arrived at Cairnryan to be broken up.

HMS CAISTOR CASTLE (June 53)

Castle class corvette built by J Lewis & Sons at Aberdeen launched 22.5.44 and completed 29.9.44. 1947 Reserve at Devonport. 1949 refitted at Barry. 1951 refitted at Falmouth. 1953 2nd Training Squadron based at Portland. 15.6.53 Coronation Review at Spithead. 1955 Reserve at Devonport. 3.56 broken up by Arnott Young & Co Ltd at Dalmuir.

HMS CAMPANIA (June 52)

Building as a fast cargo ship by Harland & Wolff at Belfast she was taken over and completed 7.3.44 as an escort aircraft carrier. Operated in Home Waters, principally defending convoys on the North Russia run, and her aircraft accounted for two U-boats, three trawlers and a number of aircraft. Post war was laid up in the Gareloch but in 1950 was lent to the Festival of Britain Organisation for use as a mobile exhibition ship visiting many ports. 10.6.52 left Portsmouth for Australia carrying the 'equipment' for the atomic bomb trials to be held at Monte Bello Island 3.10.52. 15.12.52 She returned to Portsmouth to pay off. 11.11.55 arrived at Blyth to be broken up.

HMS CAMPERDOWN (June 53)

Battle class destroyer built by Fairfield at Govan launched 8.2.44 and completed 18.6.45. 19th Destroyer Flotilla, British Pacific Fleet until 1947 then paid off into Reserve. 15.6.53 Coronation Review at Spithead. 2.10.57 recommissioned for Home/Mediterranean service with the 3rd Destroyer Squadron. 5.60 redesignated 1st Destroyer Squadron. 4.62 paid off into Reserve at Devonport. 9.70 arrived Faslane to be broken up.

HMS CARRON (October 58)

Ca class destroyer built by Scotts at Greenock launched 28.3.44 and completed 6.11.44. Joined the 6th Destroyer Flotilla in the Home Fleet operating off Norway until May when she refitted at Portsmouth. 8.45 sailed for the Far East. 5.46 returned to UK and paid off into Reserve at Chatham. 1953-55 modernised at Chatham and converted for service with the Dartmouth Training Squadron until 1960. 7.60 recommissioned as navigation training ship attached to HMS DRYAD. 29.3.63 paid off into Reserve at Portsmouth. 31.3.67 towed from Portsmouth to Inverkeithing to be broken up.

HMS CENTAUR (October 53)

Hermes class light fleet carrier built by Harland & Wolff, Belfast—laid down 30.5.44, launched 22.4.47 and completed 1.9.53. Service in Home waters and the Mediterranean was followed by a refit at Devonport in which steam catapults were installed. March 1961 a further extensive refit was completed at Portsmouth. July 1961 she took part in the reinforcement of Kuwait and carried the Royal Marines to Tanganyika in January 1964. From late 1965 to early 1970 was used as an accommodation ship at Devonport and Portsmouth. On 4.9.72 left Devonport under tow, for Cairnryan to be broken up.

HMS CEYLON (April 50)

Modified Fiji class cruiser built by Stephens at Govan launched 30.7.42 and completed 13.7.43. After two months in the Home Fleet transferred to the Eastern Fleet and took part in many carrier raids, bombardments and partols against Japanese held territory until 10.45 when she returned to the UK for refit and lay up. Recommissioned in March 1950 for 4th CS, East Indies and was actively engaged in the Korean War, carrying out a number of bombardments. Paid off at Portsmouth 10.54 for reconstruction. 1956-59 served in the Mediterranean, Home Fleet and East of Suez. 18.12.59 returned to Portsmouth and (9.2.60) transferred to the Peruvian Navy and renamed CORONEL BOLOGNESI. Deleted 1980.

HMS CHAPLET (July 59)

Ch class destroyer built by Thornycrofts at Southampton launched 18.7.44 and completed 24.8.45, joining the 14th Destroyer Flotilla for Mediterranean service. 7.50 main turbines badly damaged at Malta and had to return to UK. Paid off into Reserve. 1953 recommissioned for 1st Destroyer Squadron in the Mediterranean (fitted as minelayer). 3.12.56 returned to Portsmouth. 2.59 recommissioned at Devonport for Home service as part of the Devonport Local Squadron. 9.61 paid off into low category Reserve at Devonport. 6.11.65 arrived at Blyth to be broken up.

HMS CHARITY (April 55)

Ch class destroyer built by Thornycrofts at Southampton launched 30.11.44 and completed 19.11.45. 1946 14th Destroyer Flotilla, Mediterranean, then 1st Destroyer Flotilla, Mediterranean. 29.6.49 slightly damaged in collision with HMS/M TEREDO. 12.49 transferred to 8th Destroyer Flotilla in the Far East. Operated with Allied Forces in the Korean War. 1954 sailed home via the Mediterranean. 8.10.54 escorted HMS GAMBIA from Malta to Portsmouth, arriving 14.10.54. Paid off into Reserve. Sold to Pakistan, refitted at Cowes 1982 deleted from the Pakistan Navy List.

HMS CHEERFUL (June 53)

Algerine class minesweeper built by Harland & Wolff at Belfast launched 21.5.44 and completed 13.10.44.
Joined 18th MSF for service in Home Waters. 1947-50 Reserve. 1950-51 Refitted at Liverpool prior to joining the
4th MSF in the Channel Command. Present at the Coronation Review at Spithead 15.6.53. 9.63 Broken up at
Queenborough after nearly nine years in Reserve at Chatham.

CLEARWATER (June 52)

Built as the German Diving Vessel LUMME and completed 7.41. Taken over in 1945 and used as a tender to HMS VERNON, the Torpedo and Anti-submarine School. She was principally employed as a tender to the Deep Diving Trials Vessel RECLAIM. Sold out of service 1958.

HMS CLEOPATRA (June 53)

Dido class cruiser built by Hawthorn Leslie on the Tyne, launched 27.3.40 and completed 20.11.41. Her war service was almost entirely confined to the hectic waters of the Mediterranean until she was torpedoed and severely damaged by the Italian submarine DANDOLO on 16 July 1943 off Sicily. Left Home waters in May 1945 for the 5th CS, East Indies until early 1946, then served in the Home Fleet until 1951. A commission in the Mediterranean until early 1953, followed by the Coronation Review at Spithead in June 1953, was her last active service. Laid up at Portsmouth until broken up at Newport 1958-59.

HMS CONISTON (April 53)

Coastal minesweeper built by Thornycrofts at Woolston' launched 9.7.52 and completed 4.53 with a short funnel which was later changed to the standard type (see BADMINTON). Served in the 104th MSS until 1957 then joined the 100th MSS for two years. A period in the Operational Reserve was followed by eight years in Reserve at Hythe and Gibraltar. Sold 5.2.70 and broken up from 8.70 at Newhaven.

HMS CONTEST (August 55)

Co class destroyer built by White at Cowes launched 16.12.44 and completed 9.11.45. 1946 joined 8th Destroyer Flotilla in the Far East. 1948 returned to UK. 1949 attendant destroyer to Home Fleet aircraft carriers. 2.50 submarine target ship for boats based at Gosport. 15.6.53 Coronation Review at Spithead. 1954 refitted for minelaying. 1955 6th Destroyer Squadron on Home/Mediterranean service. 1959 paid off into Reserve at Chatham. 2.2.60 arrived at Grays to be broken up.

HMS COOK (June 51)

Built as the frigate PEGWELL BAY by Pickersgill & Sons, at Sunderland launched 24.9.45 then laid up. 1947 renamed COOK. 20.7.50 completed by Devonport Dockyard as a survey vessel. Carried out surveying in Home Waters until 1956. Refitted at Devonport and commissioned 13.3.57 for operations in the Pacific. 10.63 damaged by striking a coral reef in the Fiji Islands. 24.2.64 returned to Devonport to pay off for disposal. 1.5.68 Sold out of service.

HMS CRISPIN (June 53)

Cr class destroyer built by Whites at Cowes launched 23.6.45 as CRACCHER. Renamed 6.46 and completed 10.7.46 for service with the 4th Escort Flotilla. Later transferred to the 3rd Training Flotilla. 15.6.53 Coronation Review at Spithead representing Plymouth Command. 1954 paid off into Reserve. 2.56 sold to Pakistan and refitted at Southampton. 18.3.58 handed over to Pakistan at Southampton and renamed JAHANGIR. 1982 deleted from the Pakistan Navy List.

HMS CROSSBOW (June 53)

Weapon class destroyer built by Thornycrofts at Woolston launched 20.12.45 and completed 4.3.48. On completion joined 6th Destroyer Flotilla and took part in any Home Fleet and NATO exercises until 1955 when she paid off into Reserve. Converted into Fleet Radar Picket at Chatham from 5.57. Recommissioned 21.4.59 she served with the 2nd and 5th Destroyer Squadrons on Home/Mediterranean commissions, departing Malta for the last time 26.3.62. A refit at Chatham in 1963 was followed by a period in Reserve at Portsmouth. 1966-70 Static Harbour Training Ship attached to HMS SULTAN. 21.1.72 arrived at Briton Ferry to be broken up.

CT 8045 (May 52)

Built by Vosper. Ordered as MTB 537 2.12.43 but redesignated CT (Controlled Target) 45 in 12.45 and completed in 1948. Subsequently re-numbered CT 8045. Sold out of service 3.10.58.

HMS CUMBERLAND (June 51)

Kent class heavy cruiser built by Vickers Armstrongs at Barrow launched 16.3.26 and completed 23.1.28. 1928-34 and 1936-38 in 5th CS China Station. On South Atlantic Station at outbreak of war and witnessed the scuttling of the ADMIRAL GRAF SPEE 17.12.39. 10.41 joined 1st CS Home Fleet covering convoys to Russia until 1.44 when transferred to 4th CS Eastern Fleet. 12.11.45 returned to UK. Trooping until 6.46 then laid up. 1949-51 converted at Devonport to Trials Cruiser with all original armament removed. 1951-58 engaged in prolonged series of trials with 6" and 3" dual purpose guns, pre-wetting systems, propellers, etc. 1.59 laid up. 3.11.59 arrived Newport to be broken up.

HMS DAINTY (April 53)

Daring class destroyer built by Whites at Cowes launched 16.8.50 and completed 26.2.53. After trials and limited service was paid off and cocooned in mid 1954. Laid up at Portsmouth and Barrow. 1.56 commissioned for general Home/Mediterranean service. 1958 refitted at Portsmouth. 1959 2nd Destroyer Squadron. 21.11.60 arrived at Portsmouth to pay off. 1962-64 refitted at Portsmouth. 9.4.65 commissioned for 23rd Escort Squadron and spent the next four years travelling extensively (West Indies, East Indies, Mediterranean, Far East and Home waters). 30.7.69 arrived at Portsmouth to pay off for disposal. 1.2.70 sold for breaking up at Cairnryan.

HMS DARK CLIPPER (March 57)

Fast patrol boat built by Vosper launched 9.2.55. First commissioned 31.1.57 at HMS HORNET, Gosport. Shown fitted as a motor torpedo boat with 1 x 40mm Bofors gun and 2 torpedo tubes. 1959 reduced to Operational Reserve. 1964 placed on Sales List. Broken up at Malta.

HMS DARK KILLER (January 57)

Fast patrol boat built by Thornycroft launched 26.9.56. Shown armed with 1 x 40mm Bofors gun and 2 torpedo tubes although could carry various combinations of other weapons which included a 4.5 inch gun, ground mines and depth charges. 1959 in Operational Reserve. 1965 on Disposal List. 1967 sold to Italian customs service.

DECIBEL (January 56)

Laid down by J Bolson & Sons Ltd at Poole as the excursion vessel BOURNEMOUTH BELLE but taken over for use as an experimental trials vessel attached to HMS OSPREY at Portland. Launched 21.11.53. Used as a trials ship for underwater detection equipment and then laid up at Portsmouth. Offered for sale 'as lies' and purchased 8.58 by Dutch commercial interests. 30.8.58 arrived under tow at Amsterdam.

HMS DEFENDER (March 59)

Daring class destroyer built by Stephen at Linthouse launched 27.7.50 and completed 4.12.52. 15.6.53 Coronation Review at Spithead. 16.6.53 sailed for the Far East. 20.12.54 arrived back at Chatham. 1956 temporarily transferred to the Mediterranean during the Suez Crisis. 1958-59 refit at Chatham. 1959 2nd Destroyer Squadron on General Service commission. 1961-65 Reserve at Chatham but refitted 1962 at Rosyth. 1965 commissioned for 23rd Escort Squadron. 24.8.65 sailed from Portsmouth for the Mediterranean. 1967 recommissioned for Home/Far East service. 9.69 paid off at Devonport. 1972 broken up at Inverkeithing.

HMS DEVONSHIRE (June 53)

Heavy cruiser of London class built at Devonport Dockyard launched 22.10.27. Spent most of her early life in the Mediterranean. 11.39 Joined Home Fleet and took part in operations off Norway, the attack on Dakar and convoys to Russia. 11.41 to the South Atlantic and 22.11.41 sank German raider ATLANTIS. 1942-43 Eastern Fleet; 1944-45 Home Fleet followed by trooping duties. 9.46-4.47 refitted as Cadet Training Ship. 1947-53 in service carrying out training duties and cruises. 15.6.53 at Spithead for the Coronation Review where she was the oldest warship present. 10.53 reduced to Reserve. 12.12.54 arrived at Newport to be broken up.

RFA DEWDALE (note the deck cargo) (September 56)

Built by Cammell Laird at Birkenhead and launched 7.2.41 as a tanker but converted while under construction to a LSG (Landing Ship, Gantry). Took part in Operation Torch 11.42. In 3.43 was bombed and damaged in Algiers harbour and was not fit to return to the UK until 15.10.43. After permanent repairs returned to the Mediterranean and late in 1944 moved to the East Indies Fleet. 1946-47 converted back to tanker at Portsmouth and commenced normal freighting duties with the RFA until being sold for breaking up in Antwerp 1959.

HMS DIAMOND (May 57)

Daring class destroyer built by J Brown at Clydebank launched 14.6.50, completed 21.2.52 and joined Home Fleet. 29.9.53 bows damaged in collision with HMS SWIFTSURE off Iceland. 9.54 to the Mediterranean. 1.7.55 returned to Chatham. 11.56 Suez operations 5.57 visited the USA then joined the 5th Destroyer Squadron in the Mediterranean. 1959 refitted at Chatham. 1961 5th Destroyer Squadron then 23rd Escort Squadron. 5.63 turbines sabotaged at Chatham. 25.6.64 collided with HMS SALISBURY in the Channel. 1965-67 refit and Reserve at Chatham. 8.67 recommissioned for Home/Far East service. 12.69 paid off at Portsmouth but used as harbour training ship attached to HMS SULTAN. 9.11.81 towed to the Medway to be broken up.

DIPPER (July 50)

German boom defence training tender C 30 launched in 1943. Taken over by the Royal Navy in 1945 and renamed DIPPER in 1948. Served as a mining tender attached to HMS LOCHINVAR and HMS VERNON. 1958 in Reserve at Port Edgar. 1960 sold.

DISPENSER (May 52)

Salvage vessel built by Smiths Dock at Middlesbrough launched 22.4.43. Used on wreck clearance work. 1954 chartered to the Liverpool & Glasgow Salvage Association. 1971 returned to the Royal Maritime Auxiliary service. 1975 sold.

DIVER (September 51)

Former German Boom Defence Training Tender C28 launched 7.4.43 and taken over in 1945. Named DIVER in 1948 and principally operated as a Mine Location Vessel attached to the 1st Minesweeping Experimental Flotilla based at Port Edgar on the Forth. Sold in 1959, becoming the Italian motor vessel PEMBRIA.

HMS DUCHESS (March 54)

Daring class destroyer built by Thornycrofts at Woolston launched 9.4.51 and completed 23.10.52 for the Home Fleet. 26.1.53 boiler blow-back killed one man and injured three. 15.6.53 Coronation Review at Spithead. 1954-12.58 on Home/Mediterranean commissions. 12.58 paid off for long refit. 8.11.60 commissioned for trials. 1.61 Leader of the 5th Destroyer Squadron on Home/Mediterranean service. 1.63 joined 24th Escort Squadron for Far East commission. 6.4.64 sailed from Singapore to join the Royal Australian Navy on loan. 1972 purchased by Australia for conversion to training ship. 1977 paid off for disposal. 1980 broken up in Taiwan.

HMS EAGLE (June 53)

Fleet aircraft carrier built by Harland & Wolff at Belfast, being laid down 24.10.42, launched 19.3.46 and completed 1.10.51. Originally to be named AUDACIOUS but was renamed 21.1.46. 1.3.52 accepted into service and became Flagship of the Flag Officer, Heavy Squadron, Home Fleet. 6.11.56 took part in the Suez assault. 1959-64 major reconstruction at Devonport. 1965-66 in Indian Ocean; 1966-67 refit followed by a further commission East of Suez until 6.68. 5.3.69 her last commission commenced and took in Home, Mediterranean and Far East waters before returning to Portsmouth 26.1.72 to de-store. 8.72 towed to Devonport. 13.10.78 towed from Devonport to be broken up at Cairnryan.

HMS EXPLORER (March 57)

An unarmed experimental submarine built by Vickers Armstrongs at Barrow, launched 5.3.54 and accepted into Royal Naval service 8.5.56. Designed to test the practicalities of hydrogen-peroxide/diesel fuel combustion to drive a high speed turbine. Used as a fast underwater target for anti-submarine forces. Was to be refitted 1962 but found to be in a poor condition and laid up. 8.2.65 handed over to TW Ward Ltd at Barrow to be broken up.

HMS FLATHOLM (March 50)

Isles class trawler launched 8.5.43 and completed 20.8.43. Carried out convoy escort duties in 1944. Later converted to Wreck Dispersal Vessel and joined the 1st Wreck Dispersal Flotilla based on Rosyth. 1950 operated in the English Channel destroying the wrecks of merchant ships which included the BRITSUM (sunk 5.7.40), CORBET WOODALL (sunk 30.5.17) and ST RONAIG (sunk 11.6.40). 1955 designated a special survey vessel. 31.8.60 sold. 3.9.60 arrived under tow at Antwerp to be broken up.

RFA FORT CONSTANTINE (August 53)

Built in Canada in 1944. Operated in the Pacific as Victualling Store Issuing Ship under the management of Ellerman & Bucknall. 1950 refitted at Southampton by Thornycrofts as a Royal Fleet Auxiliary Store Carrier. Supported the atom bomb tests in the Pacific 1957-59 but more usually operated carrying naval stores between the UK and the Mediterranean. Laid up 12.62. 8.69 listed for sale 'as lies' at Plymouth and broken up at Hamburg from 12.69.

FRESHFORD (June 53)

Water carrier built by the Lytham Shipbuilding & Engineering Co Ltd and launched 23.3.44. Based at Portsmouth and operated by the Port Auxiliary Service to provide fresh water to vessels anchored in the harbour or at Spithead. Listed for sale at Portsmouth 7.67 and sold 1969.

HMS GAMBIA (October 54)

Colony class cruiser built by Swan Hunter on the Tyne; launched 30.11.40 and completed 21.2.42. In May 1942 arrived at Mombasa to join 4th CS Eastern Fleet. 6-9.43 refitted at Liverpool then transferred to Royal New Zealand Navy in place of LEANDER. 2.44 rejoined 4th CS and became part of British Pacific Fleet in 1.45. 2-5.4.45 towed the disabled destroyer ULSTER to Leyte. 2.9.45 present at the formal surrender of Japan in Tokyo Bay. 7.7.46 returned to Royal Navy control at Devonport. 1947 5th CS Pacific. 1950-54 Mediterranean Fleet, followed by service in the East Indies, Home Fleet, South Atlantic and Far East until 1960. 1961-68 in Reserve at Portsmouth. 2.12.68 left Portsmouth under tow for Inverkeiting to be broken up.

HMS GAY BOMBARDIER (April 53)

Fast patrol boat built by Vospers launched 25.8.52. The first of the class accepted into the Royal Naval service. Shown operating as a torpedo boat with a twin 20mm Oerlikon and 2 torpedo tubes. 15.6.53 Coronation Review at Spithead. 5.54 close escort to HM Royal Yacht BRITANNIA up the River Thames from the Nore. 1958 laid up at Hythe. 26.7.63 sold.

HMS GAY CENTURION (August 53)

Fast patrol boat built by Thornycroft launched 3.9.52. Shown fitted as gunboat with a short barrelled 4.5 inch gun forward and a 40mm Bofors gun aft. 1957 Reserve. 1961 on Sales List. 31.1.62 sold.

HMS GAY CHARGER (May 56)

Fast patrol boat built by Morgan Giles launched 12.1.53. 5.54 close escort to HM Royal Yacht BRITANNIA from the Nore to the Pool of London. 1955 Reserve. 1959 converted to high speed target towing vessel based at Devonport. 1964 paid off for disposal. Shown fitted with a 4.5 inch gun forward, a 40mm Bofors gun aft and 2 torpedo tubes.

HMS GIRDLE NESS (June 57)

Built in Canada as a depot ship for landing craft and launched 29.3.45. 1946-53 in Reserve at Rosyth. 1953-56 converted to a Guided Weapons Trials Ship at Devonport. 1956-61 used as test ship for Seaslug missiles, spending most of 1959-61 in the Mediterranean. 1962-70 in Reserve at Rosyth serving as base and accommodation ship. 11.8.70 arrived at Faslane to be broken up.

HMS GLASGOW (May 53)

Southampton class cruiser built by Scotts at Greenock. Launched 20.6.36 and completed 8.9.37. Served in the Home, Eastern and Mediterranean Fleets until 1945. During the war she collided with the destroyer IMOGEN which sank 16.7.40; sank the RIN vessel PRABHAVATI by mistake 9.12.41; with HMS ENTERPRISE sank the German T25, T26 and Z27 (28.12.43) in the Bay of Biscay and was damaged by a shore battery off Normandy 26.6.44. In 9.45 became Flagship of 5th CS in the East Indies and in 9.46 was Flagship of 4th CS in the same waters. Refits and West Indies service were followed by duty as Flagship of the C-in-C Mediterranean and Flagship of Flag Officer Flotillas, Home Fleet. 1956 reduced to Reserve at Portsmouth. 8.7.58 arrived Blyth to be broken up.

HMS GLORY (March 54)

Colossus class light fleet carrier built by Harland & Wolff at Belfast launched 27.11.43 and completed 2.4.45.
Joined the 11th Aircraft Carrier Squadron in the Pacific and took part in the formal surrender of the Japanese
forces in the Solomons area. Involved in repatriation duties and returned to the UK 1947 and decommissioned
until 1950. 1951-53 served in the Far East and Mediterranean, including action in the Korean War. 1954
Trooping. 1955-56 refitted then 1956-61 at Rosyth in Reserve. 8.61 arrived Inverkeithing to be broken up.

HMS GOSSAMER (June 58)

Built by Philip & Son at Dartmouth, launched 18.8.39 as the controlled minelayer M2. Renamed MINER II in 1942. Served throughout the war in Home waters laying mines to protect ports and shipping channels. Renamed GOSSAMER in 1949. Became mine location vessel attached to HMS OSPREY at Portland. c.5.70 sunk as target by the Iranian destroyer ARTEMIZ (ex-HMS SLUYS) off Portland.

HMS GREY GOOSE (June 56)

Former steam gunboat SGB 9 built by Whites at Cowes launched 14.2.42 and completed 4.7.42. 19.8.42 damaged by bomb during Dieppe Raid. 1.6.43 renamed GREY GOOSE. 27.7.43 and 4.9.43 damaged in action with enemy trawlers. 6.6.44 D-Day. 9-12.44 converted to minesweeper and based at Dover. 1946/7 laid up at Cowes then Portsmouth. 1952-54 fitted with gas turbine propulsion by Vospers. 1954 in Portsmouth Trials Squadron. 1957 reduced to Reserve, Portsmouth. 29.10.58 sold out of service with engines removed. 1.84 At Southwick to be sold by the Admiralty Marshal; partially converted to a yacht and named ANSERAVA.

HMS HELMSDALE (February 52)

River class frigate built by Inglis at Glasgow launched 5.6.43 and completed 15.10.43. Worked as convoy escort in the North Atlantic. 9.9.44 with PORTCHESTER CASTLE sank U743 near convoy ONF.252. 1947 converted at Devonport into Underwater Experimental Vessel with glass panels in the hull to study water movements. 1949 2nd Training Flotilla. 4.51 took part in the search for HMS AFFRAY. 15.6.53 One of the inspecting ships at the Coronation Review. 1954 Reserve at Devonport. 7.11.57 arrived at Faslane to be broken up.

HMS HERMES (November 59)

Aircraft carrier built by Vickers Armstrongs at Barrow. Launched 16.2.53 and commissioned 25.11.59. Work on her was suspended 1953-56. Throughout the sixties served principally in the Far East and Indian Ocean with a long refit 1964-66. From March 1971 to June 1973 was converted to a Commando Carrier then converted again 1976-77 into a combined Commando Carrier and Anti-submarine ship. In 1980-81 refitted at Portsmouth with a 'ski-jump' to enable her to operate Harrier jet aircraft. Acted as Flagship to the Task Force which recaptured the Falklands from Argentina in June 1982. Reduced to Reserve at Portsmouth.

HMS HICKLETON (August 55)

Coastal minesweeper built by Thornycrofts at Southampton launched 26.1.55 and completed 24.6.55 for service with the 108th MSS based at Malta. 1959 Malta Reserve. 1960 transferred to Reserve at Singapore. 1965/66 loaned to Royal New Zealand Navy for service in the Far East. Returned to the UK late 1966 and laid up at Hythe. 1967 sold to Argentina, refitted by Vospers and renamed NEUQUEN in 1968.

HMS ILLUSTRIOUS (July 54)

Fleet aircraft carrier built by Vickers Armstrongs at Barrow. Launched 5.4.39 and completed 21.5.40. Her war service included the famous raid on the Italian Fleet at Taranto 11.11.40. 10.1.41 Severely damaged by German bombers which put her out of action for a year. She covered the landings at Diego Suarez 5.42 and Salerno 9.43. Throughout 1944 she operated in the Indian Ocean and transferred to the Pacific in 1945 where, on 6.4.45, she was "near-missed" by a Kamikaze aircraft. Returned to the UK for a long refit until 6.46. 1946-54 used as a deck landing trials and training carrier with refits in 1948 and 1950-51. Laid up in the Gareloch until 3.11.56 when she was moved to Faslane to be broken up.

HMS IMPLACABLE (June 53)

Fleet aircraft carrier built by Fairfields at Govan launched 10.12.42 and completed 28.8.44. Carried out numerous air strikes on targets in Norwegian waters until being transferred to the British Pacific Fleet in time for strikes against Truk. 6.45 and the Japanese homelands 7 and 8.45. The end of the war meant a period in Reserve and under refit before serving for a year (1949-50) as Flagship of the C-in-C Home Fleet. 1951-54 in the Training Squadron and was present at the Spithead Review 6.53 as Flagship of the Flag Officer, Training Squadron. 1954 reduced to Reserve and in 11.55 her breaking up commenced at Inverkeithing.

HMS INDEFATIGABLE (June 53)

Fleet aircraft carrier built by John Browns on the Clyde launched 8.12.42 and completed 3.5.44. Served six months in the Home Fleet before transferring to the British Pacific Fleet 11.44. 2.9.45 In Tokyo Bay for the formal surrender of Japan then spent some months on repatriation duties. 1948-49 Reserve Fleet 1950 refitted for service as Flagship of the Training Squadron. Mid 1954 reduced to Reserve and towed to Dalmuir in late 1956 to be broken up.

HMS INGLESHAM (May 53)

The first of the post-war inshore minesweepers being built by Whites at Cowes launched 23.4.52 completed 13.5.53. After trials, served in the 50th MS Squadron based on Port Edgar until 1959. Paid off at Hythe 24.3.59 and crew transferred to HMS YAXHAM. 29.9.66 Sold for breaking up at Rotterdam.

HMS JAMAICA (May 52)

Cruiser built by Vickers Armstrongs at Barrow; launched 16.11.40 and completed 29.6.42. Commissioned for 10th CS Home Fleet and remained in Home Waters until 8.45, except for one month in late 1942 when she covered the North African landings. Principally engaged in escorting convoys to North Russia. 31.12.42 fought action against German cruiser HIPPER and destroyers. 26.12.43 assisted in the destruction of the German battlecruiser SCHARNHORST off North Cape. 6.6.45 took King George VI on a visit to the Channel Islands. 1945-47 East Indies and Mediterranean. 1949 West Indies but then transferred to the Far East because of the Yangtse incident and remained until 1.51, taking part in operations off Korea. After refit and a period in Reserve saw duty in the Home Fleet and in the Mediterranean. 1957 paid off and 12.12.60 arrived Dalmuir to be broken up.

HMS KENYA (February 53)

Colony class cruiser built by Stephens at Govan launched 18.8.39 and completed 28.8.40. Her war service took her to the Arctic, North Sea, North Atlantic, Mediterranean, South Atlantic and Indian Ocean. The highlights of this service were when she sank the German tanker KOTA PINANG 3.10.41, took part in the Vaagso Raid 27.12.41, and was torpedoed and damaged by the Italian submarine ALAGI during Operation Pedestal 12-13.8.42. Her post war service included commissions in the West Indies, Far East (including Korea) and a period in Reserve. Returned to Portsmouth for a long refit 24.2.53. Rejoined Home Fleet 11.56 after a short commission as Flagship of the C-in-C, America and West Indies Station. Paid off into Reserve 9.58 and sold for breaking up 1962.

HMS LARGO BAY (June 53)

Frigate built by Pickersgill at Sunderland, launched 3.10.44 and completed 26.1.46. Laid up in Reserve from completion to 1951 at Portsmouth. 2.52 commissioned for 4th Training Squadron based on Rosyth. 15.6.53 Coronation Review at Spithead. 1954 reduced to Reserve at Portsmouth. 11.7.58 arrived at Inverkeithing to be broken up.

HMS LINDISFARNE (August 53)

Isles class trawler built by Cook, Welton & Gemmell at Beverley launched 17.6.43 and completed 17.9.43. Fitted as anti-submarine trawler. 6.6.44 supported operations off Normandy. 1946 converted to wreck dispersal vessel for service with the 1st Wreck Dispersal Flotilla. 1950 clearing wrecks in the Bristol Channel. 26.4.58 arrived under tow at Dover to be broken up.

HMS LIVERPOOL (April 52)

Cruiser of the later Southampton class built by Fairfields at Govan. Launched 24.3.37 and completed 25.10.38. Served on the East Indies, China and Mediterranean stations until 14.10.40 when she was severely damaged by an aerial torpedo. Soon after rejoining the fleet again damaged by an aerial torpedo (14.6.42) in the Mediterranean and was under repair for the rest of the war. 1945-52 Mediterranean Fleet (Flagship of Rear Admiral The Earl Mountbatten of Burma 1949-50). 1953-58 Portsmouth Reserve. 2.7.58 arrived at Bo'ness to be broken up.

HMS LOCH ALVIE (March 54)

Frigate built by Barclay Curle at Glasgow launched 14.4.44 and completed 21.8.44. Operated with the Canadian 9th Escort Group on convoy escort duties including the last convoy to N Russia. 1946 Sheerness Reserve. 4.50 joined 6th Frigate Flotilla Home Fleet. 10.52 paid off at Portsmouth for modernisation and re-arming. 3.54 sailed for the East Indies on the first of six commissions in those waters lasting until 9.63. 11.63 paid off and cannibalised for spares at Singapore. 11.65 broken up at Singapore.

HMS LOCH FADA (November 56)

Frigate built by J Brown at Clydebank launched 14.12.43 and completed 10.4.44. Operated as convoy escort. 6.6.44 D-Day. 27.2 45 sank U1018 in SW Approaches. 28.2.45 with other ships sank U327 off the Isles of Scilly. 1946 joined A/S Training Squadron based on Londonderry. 1952 paid off for re-arming at Portsmouth. 5.55 commissioned for East Indies Station. 10.62 transferred to 2nd Destroyer Squadron, Far East. 11.10.67 returned to Portsmouth to pay off. 1.2.68 towed from Portsmouth to lay up in Luce Bay. 1970 broken up at Inverkeithing.

HMS LOCH KILLISPORT (September 59)

Frigate built by Harland & Wolff at Belfast launched 6.7.44 and completed 9.7.45. Sailed for the East Indies. 11.47 Reserve at Devonport. 4.50 6th Frigate Flotilla, Home Fleet. 1953 re-armed at Blackwall. 2.55 commissioned for East Indies Station. 14.7.57 first British warship to enter the Suez Canal since its blocking. 8.60 paid off at Portsmouth for refit. 8.61 commissioned for Far East service. 4.8.65 returned to Portsmouth to pay off for disposal. 18.3.70 arrived at Blyth to be broken up.

HMS LYSANDER (July 55)

Algerine class minesweeper built by Port Arthur Shipyards in Canada launched 11.11.43 and completed 21.11.44. In the 11th MSF until 1.47 when she paid off into Reserve at Singapore. Renamed CORNFLOWER 3.50-7.51 as RNVR ship at Hong Kong. 7.51 6th MSF at Singapore. 1954 refitted at Sheerness. 18.4.55 commissioned into VERNON Squadron as training ship. 5.56 Reserve at Chatham. 23.11.57 arrived at Blyth to be broken up.

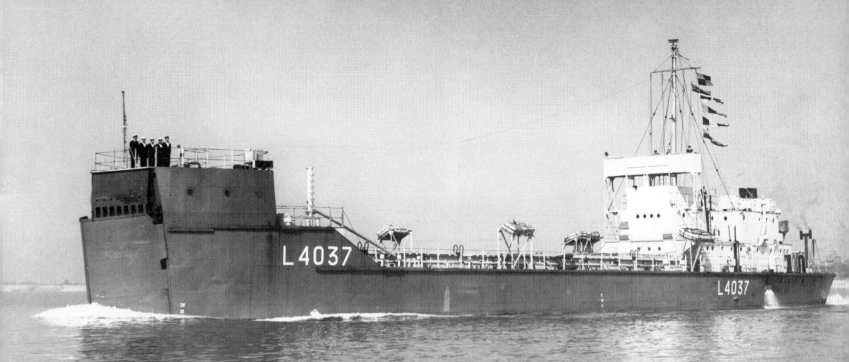

LCT 4037 (June 51)

Tank landing craft built in 1945 by Sir Wm. Arrol at Alloa. Intended for Far Eastern service. 4.53 listed in Category II Reserve. 1956 renamed RAMPART. 8.65 paid off to Reserve, Portsmouth. 1966 transferred to War Department—Royal Corps of Transport, and renamed AKYAB after refit at Devonport. c.1974 deleted from service. Ultimate fate unknown.

LCT 4039 (March 54)

Tank landing craft built in 1945 by Sir Wm. Arrol at Alloa. 4.53 listed in Category II Reserve. 15.6.53 Coronation Review at Spithead. 1956 renamed PARAPET when in the Mediterranean. 9.60 commissioned at Malta for service East of Suez. 1966 sold to La Societe Meseline Ltd. (Merchants), Sark.

HMS MAGPIE (March 55)

Sloop built by Thornycroft at Southampton. Launched 24.3.43 and completed 30.8.43. A member of Captain Walker's famous 2nd Support Group and took part in the destruction of U592 (31.1.44) and U238 (9.2.44). 6.44 supported the Normandy operations. 1946 2nd Frigate Flotilla, Mediterranean. 2.9.50 the first command of HRH The Duke of Edinburgh. 1.10.54 returned to Portsmouth. 1955 South Atlantic Squadron. 10.58 stripped at Devonport. 12.7.59 arrived at Blyth to be broken up.

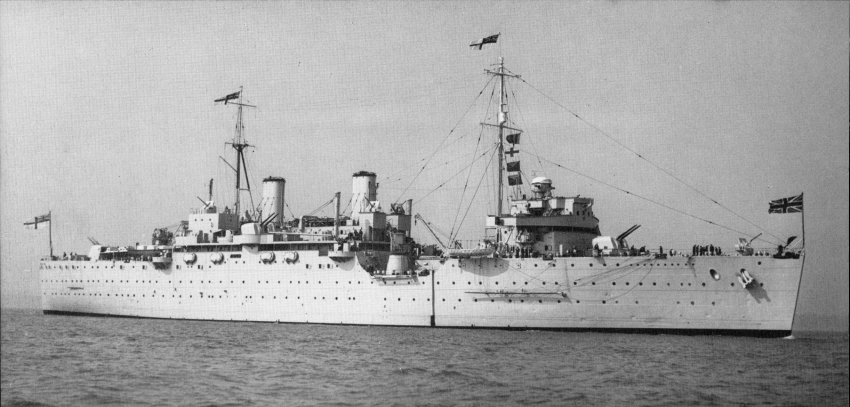

HMS MAIDSTONE (June 52)

Submarine Depot Ship built by John Browns at Clydebank launched 21.10.37 and completed 5.5.38. During the war served in the Mediterranean, South Atlantic, Home Fleet, Eastern Fleet and Pacific Fleet. The remainder of her operational career was in Home Waters except for the occasional cruise. 16.8.56 to 4.58 was Flagship of C-in-C, Home Fleet. 31.3.58 arrived at Portsmouth. Reconstructed before recommissioning 1.5.62. Based at Faslane with refits at Rosyth until 8.68 when she returned to Portsmouth. 10.69 to 1977 used as Army accommodation ship and then prison ship at Belfast. 23.5.78 arrived Inverkeithing to be broken up.

HMS MANXMAN (August 51)

Fast minelayer built by Stephen at Linthouse launched 5.9.40 and completed 20.6.41. Until 10.42 operated in Home and Mediterranean waters. 1.12.42 torpedoed by U375 off Oran—repairs took until 4.45. 6.45 sailed for the Pacific, serving there until 12.47. 1.48 Paid off at Sheerness. 27.8.51 recommissioned for the Mediterranean. 1960-63 converted to Minesweeping Support Ship at Chatham. 1963-68 Supporting the 6th MS Squadron in Far East Waters. 1969-70 Engineering Officers' Training Ship. 9.70 Paid off. 3.10.71 towed from Chatham to be broken up at Newport.

HMS MARVEL (August 53)

Algerine class minesweeper built by Redfern Construction Co in Canada launched 30.8.44 and completed
2.4.45. Part of the 3rd MSF based on Rosyth and Londonderry until transferred to the 1st MSF in 1947. Refitted
by C Hill at Bristol 1948-49 and by C Howson on Merseyside 1951. Attached to HMS VERNON and present at
the Coronation Review at Spithead 15.6.53. 7.5.58 arrived under tow at Charlestown to be broken up.

HMS MERMAID (June 53)

Sloop built by Denny at Dumbarton launched 11.11.43 and completed 12.5.44. 6.44 supported the Normandy operations. 24.8.44 assisted in the destruction of U354 and 2.9.44 of U394. 1946 2nd Frigate Flotilla, Mediterranean. 2.51 became leader of the 2nd F.F. 15.6.53 Coronation Review at Spithead. 10.8.54 returned to Portsmouth to pay off. 1958 refitted on the Tyne. 5.5.59 handed over to the Federal German Navy at Jarrow. 28.5.59 renamed SCHARNHORST and commissioned as training frigate. 30.9.72 deleted. 1974 reduced to training hulk for the Ship Safety School. Still in service, as such, 1985.

HMS MEON (June 53)

River class frigate built by Inglis at Glasgow launched 4.8.43 and completed 31.12.43. 4.44 loaned to Canadian Navy and served in the 9th Support and Escort Group. 4-12.45 converted to Landing Ship Headquarters (Small) at Southampton. 1946-51 Reserve. 3.4.51 commissioned for training. 1.5.52 allocated to the Amphibious Warfare Squadron. 15.6.53 Coronation Review at Spithead. Served in Persian Gulf area with refits at Malta until 1965. 8.7.65 arrived Portsmouth to pay off. 13.5.66 left Portsmouth under tow to be broken up at Blyth.

HMS MESSINA (May 53)

Tank landing ship built by Scotts at Greenock launched 27.4.45 as LST 3043. Re-named MESSINA in 1947. Operated in the Mediterranean and Persian Gulf and represented the Mediterranean Fleet Amphibious Warfare Squadron at the 1953 Coronation Review. 1957 detached to take part in Operation Grapple—the Christmas Island A-bomb tests. 15.5.58 returned to Chatham. 1.59 recommissioned for further service East of Suez. 7.7.65 arrived Portsmouth to pay off. 1969 transferred to Devonport for use as a store hulk. 13.10.80 towed from Plymouth to Vigo to be broken up.

HMS MINER IV (June 58)

Built by Philip & Son at Dartmouth, launched 6.8.40 as the controlled minelayer M4. Renamed MINER IV in 1942. Operated throughout the war in laying protective mine barrages in Home waters. Attached to the VERNON Flotilla for mining trials. 12.61 reported for disposal. 3.62 de-equipped at Portsmouth. 1965 sold—the first of the class to be removed from service.

HMS MONTCLARE (June 53)

Former Canadian Pacific passenger liner launched in 1921 and requisitioned 28.8.39 as an Armed Merchant Cruiser. Purchased 1942 and converted to a Destroyer Depot Ship, serving with the British Pacific Fleet 1944-45. Converted to a Submarine Depot Ship just after the war and served the 3rd Submarine Flotilla based on Rothesay. 2.55 towed to Portsmouth for refit; broke adrift off the Isles of Scilly but tow reconnected and arrived 10.2.55. Refit cancelled and laid up. 28.1.58 left Portsmouth under tow for Inverkeithing to be broken up.

MOORFOWL (September 53)

Mooring vessel built by Bow, McLachlan at Paisley and launched 11.9.19. Used on all forms of boom work, mooring and salvage, being fitted with salvage pumps, air compressors and diving equipment. Sold out of service c.1963.

HMS MYNGS (September 50)

Zambesi class destroyer built by Vickers Armstrongs on the Tyne launched 31.5.43 and completed 23.6.44. Operated in Home waters on Russian convoy duty and strikes off Norway until transferring to the East Indies Fleet. 6.46 Leader of the 4th Destroyer Flotilla, Home Fleet. 1948 3rd Escort Flotilla. 1949 2nd Training Flotilla based at Portland. 29.4.49 slightly damaged by dummy torpedo off the Isle of Wight. 15.6.53 Coronation Review at Spithead. 9.54 reduced to Reserve. 5.55 sold to Egypt as EL QAHER and refitted at Cowes. 26.8.56 sailed for Egypt. 16.5.70 sunk by Israeli aircraft at Berenice.

HMS MULL OF GALLOWAY (October 55)

Maintenance and Repair Ship built in Canada and launched 26.10.44. Served as part of the British Pacific Fleet. 1947-49 Headquarters Ship of the Senior Officer, Reserve Fleet, Clyde. 1950-54 Decommissioned and laid up. 1954 recommissioned and refitted as Inshore Minesweeping Flotilla Headquarters Ship. 1957 reduced to Reserve at Portsmouth. 16.2.65 left Portsmouth under tow to be broken up at Hamburg.

MFV 1197 (January 57)

Built c.1945 for use as a general tender. One of a large class known as the Admiralty 75ft type, of which some 250 were completed. Fate unknown but out of service by 1969.

MFV 1239 (October 58)

Motor fishing vessel of the numerous Admiralty 75′ type built 1943-45. She was built by Philip & Son at Dartmouth and was a tender attached to HMS ST VINCENT when this photograph was taken. Out of service by 1969.

ML 2912 (May 52)

A Fairmile 'B' class motor launch completed 22.7.44 as ML 912. c.1946 became ML 6007 when attached to the Rhine Flotilla. c.1950 renumbered ML 2912. Converted to inshore minesweeper. Sold out of service 15.9.58.

MMS 1044 (April 53)

Motor minesweeper launched 30.12.43 and completed 2.8.44. After sweeping duties in European waters she was transferred, on loan, to the Danish Navy from 6.45 to 11.50. Returned to the Royal Navy at Chatham and based there until 1952 when transferred to Portsmouth. Re-allocated to Chatham 1953 until sold out of service 25.11.54.

MMS 1609 (June 53)

Motor minesweeper launched 30.4.42 (as MMS 109) and completed 12.10.42. Wartime sweeping duties in Home Waters gave way to service in the Sheerness-based 101st MSF in 1946. 1947-50 based at Chatham and renumbered MMS 1609. 5.50 joined 301st Auxiliary MSF as danlayer, transferring to the 51st MSF in 1951. Moved to Rosyth 1954. 8.56 sold to Pounds of Portsmouth.

MMS 1807 (June 53)

Motor minesweeper launched 1.9.43 (as MMS 307) and completed 8.12.43. Loaned to Danish Navy 6.44 to 12.48.
1949-51 based at Chatham and from 1952 at Portland. Laid up at Chatham 1955. Sold 21.11.56.

MTB 1029 (June 51)

2.12.43 ordered from Vospers as MGB 529 but completed 23.5.46 as MTB 529. 1949 redesignated MTB 1029.
Shown armed with a 20mm Oerlikon gun and 2 torpedo tubes. 1953 reduced to Category III Reserve and hulked.
No further details known.

MTB 1033 (February 53)

2.12.43 ordered from Vospers as MGB 533 and completed 5.12.45 as MTB 533. 1949 redesignated MTB 1033.
Shown armed as gunboat with a 17 pdr gun forward and 2 x 20mm Oerlikon guns aft. 1953-4 renumbered FC 42
(Fleet Craft) for subsidiary service. 21.10.58 sold out of service.

MTB 5020 (September 53)

Modified Fairmile 'D' type motor torpedo boat built by Osborne at Littlehampton and completed 12.44. 4.53 In Category I Reserve. 15.6.53 Coronation Review at Spithead. 1955 converted to Coastal Forces Leader. 12.56 listed for disposal. 18.9.58 sold.

MTB 5031 (February 53)

Fairmile 'D' type motor torpedo boat (known as dogs) built by Robertson at Sandbank and completed 10.44 as MTB 758. 1949 renumbered MTB 5031. Shown armed with 2 x 17 pdr guns, 2 x 20mm Oerlikon guns and 2 torpedo tubes. Sold 14.6.56.

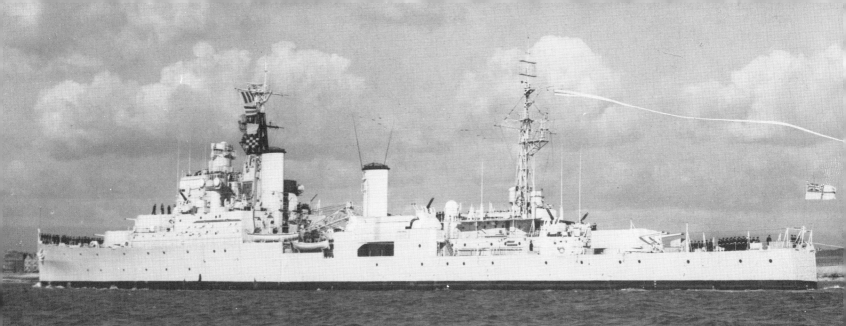

HMS NEWFOUNDLAND (February 55)

Colony class cruiser built by Swan Hunter on the Tyne launched 19.12.41 and completed 31.12.42. Joined the fleet 22.1.43 and served in the Mediterranean until 23.7.43 when she was torpedoed by the Italian submarine ASCIANGHI. Under repair until 12.44 then allocated to the Pacific. Was present at the Japanese surrender in Tokyo Bay 2.9.45. Returned to the UK 11.46. Under refit and in Reserve until 11.52. 1953-54 East Indies. 17.2.55 arrived back at Portsmouth to recommission for further East Indies service. 1.11.56 one man killed and five wounded in action in the Gulf of Suez when she sank the Egyptian frigate DOMIAT. 24.6.59 returned to Portsmouth and paid off. 30.12.59 handed over to the Peruvian Navy at Portsmouth and renamed ALMIRANTE GRAU. 1973 renamed CAPITAN QUINONES. Deleted 1979.

HMS OBDURATE (September 52)

Onslow class destroyer built by Denny at Dumbarton launched 19.2.42 and completed 3.9.42. Operated with Home Fleet escorting convoys to Russia. 31.12.42 damaged by German heavy cruiser LUTZOW and 25.1.44 damaged by T5 torpedo from U360. 1946 Torpedo training ship at Portsmouth. 2.48 reduced to Reserve. 27.10.49 towed from Harwich for refit on the Tyne then back to Reserve. 1952 commissioned for Nore Local Squadron. 15.6.53 Coronation Review at Spithead. 1957 Reserve at Portsmouth. 4.59 arrived at Rosyth for tests by the Naval Constructional Research Establishment. 30.11.64 hulk arrived at Inverkeithing to be broken up.

HMS OCEAN (September 57)

Colossus class light fleet carrier built by Stephens at Govan on the Clyde launched 8.7.44 and completed 30.6.45. Until early 1952 she operated principally in the Mediterranean and in 1949 was Flagship of the Second-in-Command, Mediterranean Fleet. 1952 Saw action in the later stages of the Korean War before being converted for service in the Training Squadron. 1958 Reduced to Reserve. 6.5.62 Arrived at Faslane to be broken up.

HMS ODIHAM (September 56)

Inshore minesweeper built by Vospers launched 21.7.55 and completed 27.7.56. On completion carried out a series of trials and was then placed on a land cradle at Rosneath, and remained there until (1964) being brought forward from Reserve for service with the Royal Naval Auxiliary Service. 1975 paid off. 1979 listed for disposal. 5.80 sold to Sutton & Smith Ltd.

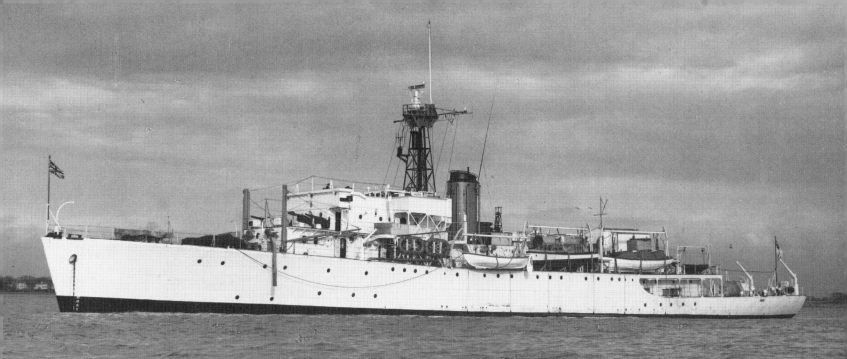

HMS OWEN (November 53)

Laid down as Bay class frigate by Hall, Russell at Aberdeen; launched 19.10.45 then laid up. Towed to Chatham and 1947 commenced completion as survey ship. 8.49 Commissioned. Carried out surveying duties in the Persian Gulf, Mediterranean, South Atlantic, Indian Ocean and Home Waters until 1965 with regular returns to the UK for refits although her biggest refit in 1959-60 was at Gibraltar. 29.9.65 arrived Devonport to pay off into Extended Reserve. 15.7.70 left Devonport under tow to be broken up at Blyth.

HMS PEACOCK (June 53)

Sloop built by Thornycrofts at Woolston launched 11.12.43 and completed 10.5.44. Joined 22nd Escort Group and assisted in the sinking of 3 U-boats; U354 (24.8.44), U394 (2.9.44) and U482 (16.1.45). 1945 joined 2nd Frigate Flotilla, Mediterranean. Except for her presence at the Coronation Review she remained in the Mediterranean until 10.8.54 when she arrived at Portsmouth, with HMS MERMAID, to pay off into Reserve. 7.5.58 arrived under tow at Rosyth to be broken up.

HMS PERSEUS (March 52)

An aircraft maintenance ship built by Vickers Armstrongs on the Tyne launched 26.3.44 and completed 8.45. After a short spell of duty in the Pacific Fleet she paid off into Reserve at Portsmouth. 1949-51 Refitted and equipped with a powerful steam driven catapult. A period of extensive trials followed and in 1953 was designated a ferry carrier. 1955 Refitted but then reduced to Reserve. 6.5.58 sold to Smith & Houston to be broken up at Port Glasgow.

HMS PELLEW (March 57)

Type 14 frigate built by Swan Hunter on the Tyne launched 29.9.54 and completed 26.7.56. Her complete operational career was spent in Home Waters attached to the 2nd Training Squadron based on Portland until 1961 when she paid off for an extended refit at Rosyth. 20.9.62 commissioned for trials then joined the 2nd Frigate Squadron, again based on Portland. 1.4.69 paid off at Portsmouth for disposal. 17.5.71 arrived at Fleetwood to be broken up.

HMS PICKLE (June 53)

Algerine class minesweeper built by Harland & Wolff at Belfast, launched 19.8.43 and completed 15.10.43. Operated in European waters until 3.45 and present at the D-Day Landings. 1945 East Indies Station. 1946 Reserve at Plymouth. 4.51 with 4th MSF in Operational Reserve at Harwich. 15.6.53 Coronation Review at Spithead. 1954 Channel Command, still with the 4th MSF, followed by Reserve at Portsmouth. 30.7.58 towed from Portsmouth to Devonport and sold to Ceylon. 6.4.59 handed over to the Royal Ceylon Navy at Devonport and renamed PARAKRAMA. Broken up 1964.

HMS PORPOISE (May 59)

Built by Vickers Armstrongs at Barrow launched 25.4.56 and completed 17.4.58, the first operational fleet submarine designed since the war to be accepted into service. 25.8.64 commenced long refit at Devonport. 1978 strengthened for use as an underwater weapons target ship. Paid off for disposal 1984-5 converted for use as a target.

HMS PORTCHESTER CASTLE (June 52)

Castle class corvette built by Swan Hunter at Wallsend-on-Tyne launched 21.6.43 and completed 8.11.43. Operated in the North Atlantic; 9.9.44 assisted HMS HELMSDALE to sink U743 and 11.11.44 with other ships sank U1200. 1947 Harwich Reserve. 1951 2nd Training Squadron based on Portland. 1953 scenes for the film "The Cruel Sea" shot on board. 11.56 Devonport Reserve. 15.5.58 while in tow of tug BRIGADIER broke adrift but later brought into Milford Haven. 17.5.58 arrived Dalmuir to be broken up.

HMS PROTECTOR (June 53)

Netlayer built by Yarrows at Glasgow launched 20.8.36 and completed 12.36. 1939 in South Atlantic. 1940 in Home Waters during early part of Norwegian campaign transferring to the Mediterranean in 5.40. 1942-45 at Bombay under repair. In Reserve until 1954 but 15.6.53 present at the Coronation Review at Spithead. 1954-5 converted into an Ice Patrol Ship at Devonport. 3.10.55 sailed from Portsmouth for her first season in the Antarctic, returning 22.5.56. Annual visits took place until she returned to Portsmouth from the Antarctic on 3.5.68 to pay off for disposal. Broken up at Inverkeithing from 3.70.

HMS RATTLESNAKE (June 53)

Algerine class minesweeper built by Lobnitz at Renfrew launched 23.2.43 and completed 23.6.43. Operated in Northern European Waters including the D-Day operations until 10.47 when she paid off into Reserve at Portsmouth. After refit joined the 4th MSF at Portland 5.51 moving on to Harwich. 10.52 joined the Fishery Protection Squadron until 1956 then paid off to Reserve. 10.59 broken up at Grangemouth.

HMS REDPOLE (July 59)

Modified Black Swan class escort sloop built by Yarrows at Scotstoun launched 25.2.43 and completed 6.43. 1943-44 operated in the Atlantic as convoy escort. 6.6.44 covered movements of assault convoys in Operation Neptune. 21.1.45 assisted in the assault on Ramree Island, Burma. 1949 completed conversion to Tender for the Navigation School. 15.6.53 acted as Admiralty Yacht at the Coronation Review. 7.5.56 slightly damaged in collision with the Danish Royal Yacht DANNEBROG at Copenhagen. 12.5.57 collided with and badly damaged the Gosport ferry VADNE at Portsmouth. 20.11 60 arrived at St David's-on-Forth to be broken up.

HMS RELENTLESS (July 51)

Rotherham class destroyer built by J Brown at Clydebank launched 15.7.42 and completed 30.11.42. Joined 11th Destroyer Flotilla in the East Indies for the duration of the war. 25.7.44 shelled Sabang. 7.46 reduced to Reserve. 1949 began conversion to Type 15 frigate at Portsmouth. 7.51 conversion completed and joined Plymouth Command after extensive trials. 15.6.53 Coronation Review at Spithead. 27.10.54 damaged in collision with HMS VIGILANT in the Minches. 1955 refitted. 1956 reduced to Reserve. 27.6.64 29th Escort Squadron. 12.64 26th Escort Squadron. 8.65 paid off for disposal. 1971 broken up at Inverkeithing.

HMS ROEBUCK (November 57)

Rotherham class destroyer built by Scotts at Greenock launched 10.12.42 and completed 10.6.43. Joined the 11th Destroyer Flotilla in the East Indies. 1946 care and maintenance at Devonport. 1949 Plymouth Local Flotilla. 1950 2nd Training Flotilla. 1951-53 converted to Type 15 frigate at Devonport. 1953-56 5th Frigate Squadron, Mediterranean. 11.7.56 arrived Devonport to pay off. 1957 refitted as training ship. 11.57 joined Dartmouth Training Squadron. 5.60 17th Escort Squadron. 10.62 paid off. 1968 towed to Rosyth and (16.7.68) damaged during target trials in Firth of Forth. 8.8.68 arrived at Inverkeithing to be broken up.

RFA SALVICTOR (July 50)

Ocean salvage vessel launched 11.3.44 at Renfrew. 8.45 attached to the British Pacific Fleet. 1950 surveyed wreck of the ROYAL OAK at Scapa. 6.52 arrived at Singapore from Portsmouth to help salve Admiralty Floating Dock No 9, sunk during the war. 1957 Christmas Island Nuclear Tests. 1963 Reserve. 11.5.66 arrived Devonport from Pembroke Dock towed by the tug SEA GIANT for a short refit. 4.7.66 Returned to S Wales to be laid up. 7.70 arrived Briton Ferry to be broken up.

HMS SCOTT (June 53)

Halcyon class built by Caledon S B Co at Dundee launched 23.8.38 and completed 13.2.39 as a survey ship but converted to minesweeper in late 1939. Operated in Home Waters gaining Battle Honours—Norway 1941 and Normandy 1944. 1946 refitted at Sheerness then undertook surveying duties in Home Waters for the next eighteen years. 15.6.53 Coronation Review at Spithead. 27.11.64 arrived Portsmouth to pay off for disposal. Arrived Troon 3.7.65 to be broken up.

HMS SEA DEVIL (February 1952)

'S' class submarine built by Scotts at Greenock. Launched 30.1.45 and completed 12.5.45. Allocated to the British Pacific Fleet. 4.48 completed refit. 15.6.53 Coronation Review at Spithead. Operated in Home and Mediterranean waters until 4.6.62 when she returned to Gosport from the Mediterranean to pay off, being the last 'S' class submarine in the active fleet. 15.12.65 towed from Portsmouth to be broken up at Newhaven.

HMS SENTINEL (March 59)

'S' class submarine built by Scotts at Greenock. Launched 27.7.45 and completed 28.12.45. 1951 joined Mediterranean Fleet. 15.6.53 Coronation Review at Spithead. 1.59 recommissioned at Chatham for the Portland Squadron. 1961 paid off. 28.2.62 sold to be broken up at Gillingham.

HMS SERAPH (July 55)

'S' class submarine built by Vickers Armstrongs at Barrow. Launched 25.10.41 and completed 10.6.42 (as P219) and joined the 8th Flotilla in the Mediterranean. 10.42 landed General Mark Clark on North African Coast. 6.11.42 brought General Giraud off from coast of South France. 1943 named SERAPH. 30.4.43 landed Major Martin (The Man Who Never Was) on Spanish Coast. 10.7.43 beacon vessel for Operation Husky. 1947 refitted for use as a target. 1963 paid off at Gosport and de-equipped. 14.12.65 towed from Portsmouth (with HMS SEA SCOUT) by the tug CYCLONE. 15.12.65 broke adrift but tow later reconnected. 20.12.65 arrived at Briton Ferry to be broken up.

HMS SHEFFIELD (June 57)

Southampton class cruiser built by Vickers Armstrongs on the Tyne. Launched 23.7.36 and completed 25.8.37. Served in the Home and Mediterranean Fleets throughout the war, taking part in actions which resulted in the sinking of the German warships BISMARCK, FRIEDRICH ECKHOLDT and SCHARNHORST. Covered numerous convoys to North Russia and Malta. After the war served three commissions as Flagship of the C-in-C, America & West Indies Station and one commission as Flagship of the Flag Officer, Heavy Squadron, Home Fleet. 1960-67 in Reserve at Portsmouth. Broken up at Faslane from 9.67.

HMS SIDON (July 50)

'S' class submarine built by Cammell Laird at Birkenhead. Launched 4.9.44 and completed 23.11.44. 1945 Pacific Fleet. 1946 Home Fleet. 15.6.53 Coronation Review at Spithead. 1954 refitted by Cammell Laird. 16.6.55 torpedo exploded while alongside HMS MAIDSTONE at Portland and boat sank with the loss of 13 lives. 23.6.55 raised. 14.6.57 towed out of Portland and sunk for further use as a target.

HMS SLEUTH (September 53)

'S' class submarine built by Cammell Laird at Birkenhead. Launched 6.7.44 and completed 8.10.44. 1945 Pacific Fleet. 11.45 returned to Portsmouth. 1946 refitted and streamlined to give higher underwater speed. 13.6.52 damaged in collision with the anchored destroyer HMS ZEPHYR at Portland. 15.9.58 arrived at Charlestown to be broken up.

HMS SOLEBAY (May 59)

Battle class destroyer built by Hawthorn Leslie at Hebburn-on-Tyne launched 22.2.44 and completed 11.10.45. Leader of the 5th Destroyer Flotilla, Home Fleet from completion until 1953. 15.6.53 Coronation Review at Spithead. 7.53 paid off into Reserve at Chatham. 5.57 joined 1st Destroyer Squadron (as leader) on Home/ Mediterranean service. 5.59 deployed to the Far East returning 4.60 for a further Home/Mediterranean commission. 9.4.62 returned to Portsmouth and became harbour training ship in place of VIGO. 7.8.67 left Portsmouth under tow to Troon to be broken up.

HMS SPARROW (May 55)

Sloop built by Denny at Dumbarton launched 18.2.46 and completed 16.12.46 for the America & West Indies Station. 4.49 to 7.49 under refit at Devonport. 15.4.51 returned again to Devonport to recommission. 22.8.51 arrived at Jamaica for hurricane relief work. 6-9.52 in the Home Fleet before serving in the 3rd Frigate Squadron in the Far East and then in the South Atlantic. 14.2.55 returned to Devonport to recommission for service in the South Atlantic. 1956 reduced to Reserve at Portsmouth. 26.5.58 arrived under tow at Rosyth to be broken up.

HMS SPRINGER (May 55)

'S' class submarine built by Cammell Laird at Birkenhead. Launched 14.5.45 and completed 2.8.45. 4.52 refitted with Snort and 4in gun removed. 15.6.53 Coronation Review at Spithead. 1955 2nd Submarine Squadron. 1.57 Home Fleet Spring Cruise to the Mediterranean. 9.10.58 transferred to Israel at Gosport and renamed TANIN. Refitted by Cammell Laird until 8.59. Trials in UK waters until 12.59 before delivery to Israel. 1968 cannibalised for spares. 1972 deleted.

HMS ST JAMES (June 53)

Battle class destroyer built by Fairfield at Govan launched 7.6.45 and completed 12.7.46. In 5th Destroyer Flotilla, Home Fleet from completion. 15.6.53 Coronation Review at Spithead then paid off into Reserve at Devonport. 2.58 commenced refit at Devonport but work cancelled 11.58 and ship stripped for disposal although £288,388 had been spent on her. 19.3.61 arrived under tow at Newport to be broken up.

HMS ST KITTS (June 53)

Battle class destroyer built by Swan Hunter on the Tyne launched 4.10.44 and completed 21.1.46. Joined 5th Destroyer Flotilla, Home Fleet. 15.6.53 Coronation Review at Spithead then paid off into Reserve. 1954 replaced VIGO in the 3rd Destroyer Squadron, Mediterranean Fleet. 11.56 took part in the Suez Canal operations. 19.12.56 returned to Devonport for Home Fleet service. 2.10.57 replaced by CAMPERDOWN and paid off into Reserve. 19.2.62 arrived at Sunderland to be broken up.

HMS STICKLEBACK (May 55)

Midget submarine built by Vickers Armstrongs at Barrow and launched 1.10.54. Used to test harbour defences. 1957-58 refitted. 15.7.58 handed over to the Royal Swedish Navy and renamed SPIGGEN. Handed back 1975 (Brought from Sweden aboard RFA RESURGENT) and now (1985) on display at the Imperial War Museum, Duxford.

HMS STRIKER (December 52)

Tank landing ship built in Canada and launched 15.2.45 as LST 3516. Renamed STRIKER 1947. 12.12.52 arrived Portsmouth from the Mediterranean (see photo) after service with the Amphibious Warfare Squadron. 15.6.53 Coronation Review at Spithead representing Portsmouth Home Command. 1960 Amphibious Warfare Squadron East of Suez. 1962 and 1965 refitted at Gibraltar. 19.6.66 arrived Portsmouth to pay off. 15.1.71 towed from Portsmouth to Valencia to be broken up.

HMS STURDY (June 55)

'S' class submarine built by Cammell Laird at Birkenhead. Launched 30.9.43 and completed 29.12.43. Operated in the East Indies and during several patrols sank well over 30 Japanese small craft. Mid-1945 returned to the UK. 1950 1st Submarine Flotilla, Mediterranean Fleet followed by the 2nd Submarine Squadron, Home Fleet. 7.57 discarded at Malta. 9.5.58 arrived on the Tyne under tow to be broken up.

HMS SUPERB (June 53)

Minotaur class cruiser built by Swan Hunter on the Tyne. Launched 31.8.43 and completed 16.11.45. Commissioned 12.45 for service with the Home Fleet. 1947 and 1949-50 flagship of 2nd CS. 1950-51 Flag of C-in-C America & West Indies Station, again in 1953 and 1955. In 1952, 1954 and 1957 Flagship of Flag Officer Flotillas, Home Fleet. 1956-57 in 4th CS East Indies. Laid up in the Gareloch late 1957. 8.8.60 arrived Dalmuir to be broken up.

HMS SURPRISE (April 53)

Ex Bay class frigate, built by Smith's Dock Co, South Bank-on-Tees. Launched 14.3.45 and completed 9.9.46 as Despatch Vessel to the Commander-in-Chief, Mediterranean and served as such until 1964—with just one visit to the UK during that time. 1953 converted to temporary Royal Yacht at Portsmouth. 15.6.53 Coronation Review at Spithead. 14.12.64 arrived Portsmouth to pay off. 26.6.65 left Portsmouth under tow for Bo'ness to be broken up.

HMS SWIFTSURE (June 53)

Cruiser built by Vickers Armstrongs on the Tyne launched 4.2.43 and completed 22.6.44. Joined the Home Fleet on completion but late in 1944 transferred to the East Indies and Pacific as Flagship of 4th CS. 16.9.45 Surrender of Japanese in Hong Kong signed on board. 11.46-4.50 in reserve and refitting. 5.50-1953 in Home Fleet including service as Flagship of Flag Officer Flotillas. During 9.53, while taking part in Exercise Mariner, was damaged in collision with HMS DIAMOND off Iceland and suffered 32 casualties. Refitted then laid up. 1956 commenced reconstruction at Chatham but (9.59) work stopped. 1960 on disposal list. 17.10.62 arrived Inverkeithing to be broken up.

HMS TABARD (July 55)

'T' class submarine built by Scotts at Greenock. Launched 21.11.45 and completed 25.6.46. Joined 1st Submarine Flotilla. 7.50 refitted at Malta (main steering cable sabotaged). 1953 commenced reconstruction. 1955 reconstruction completed and joined Home Fleet. 17.9.60 sailed from Malta to join 4th Submarine Squadron at Sydney, Australia. 8.5.63 damaged in collision with Australian frigate QUEENBOROUGH off Jervis Bay. 22.3.68 sailed for the UK via Panama. 11.6.68 arrived Portsmouth to pay off for use as static display ship at Fort Blockhouse. 12.3.74 towed from Portsmouth to Newport to be broken up.

HMS TALENT (February 56)

'T' class submarine built by Vickers Armstrongs at Barrow launched 13.2.45 and completed 26.7.45. 1949 1st Submarine Flotilla, Mediterranean Fleet. 4.50 carried out Gravity Tests for the Royal Society in the Eastern Mediterranean. 15.6.53 Coronation Review at Spithead. 15.12.54 swept out of No 3 Dry Dock at Chatham when caisson collapsed; 4 men lost. 1955 reconstructed. 8.5.56 fin damaged in collision with unknown vessel while submerged off the Isle of Wight. 1960-61 refitted at Malta. 1962 2nd Submarine Squadron. 1964 1st Submarine Squadron. 12.66 paid off and used as a harbour training boat. 28.2.70 arrived Troon to be broken up.

HMS TEAZER (August 55)

Troubridge class destroyer built by Cammell Laird at Birkenhead launched 7.1.43 and completed 13.9.43. Joined 24th Destroyer Flotilla in the Mediterranean and took part in the landings in South France 8.44 and the occupation of the Aegean Islands. 1945 transferred to the Pacific Fleet. 1946 reduced to Reserve at Devonport. 1953-54 converted to Type 16 frigate at Cardiff. 12.58 commissioned at Chatham for service with the 2nd Training Squadron. 4.61 Reserve. De-equipped at Chatham. 7.8.65 arrived at Dalmuir to be broken up.

NATIONAL · SERVICE
1956 · 1958
Alg. Reynolds

HMS THESEUS (April 53)

Colossus class light fleet carrier built by Fairfields at Govan. Launched 6.7.44 and completed 9.1.46. 1947 Flagship of Flag Officer (Air) in the Far East followed by duty as Flagship of the 3rd Aircraft Carrier Squadron. Actively engaged in operations against Chinese forces in the Korean War until 1952 when she became Flagship of the Flag Officer, Heavy Squadron and Flag Officer Commanding 2nd Aircraft Carrier Squadron, Home Fleet. 1954-57 in the Training Squadron including a year as Flagship. 1958-62 Reserve. 1962 broken up at Inverkeithing.

HMS TIGER (April 59)

Cruiser built by John Brown at Clydebank. Laid down (as BELLEROPHON) 1.10.41, launched 25.10.45 but in 7.46 construction suspended and vessel laid up. 10.54 Work recommenced to a modified design. 18.3.59 Completed. Operated in Home and Far East waters until 1968 when she was taken in hand for conversion to a command helicopter cruiser at Devonport. When completed in 1972 the conversion had cost more than her original building. 6.77 Flagship of the Flag Officer, Second Flotilla at the Silver Jubilee Review, Spithead. 20.4.78 Paid off into Portsmouth Reserve. 1985 awaiting disposal at Portsmouth.

HMS TIPTOE (August 50)

'T' class submarine built by Vickers Armstrongs at Barrow launched 25.2.44 and completed 13.6.44. The name was chosen by Winston Churchill. In the East Indies and Pacific Fleets. 1950 2nd Submarine Flotilla, Home Fleet. 1954-55 reconstructed and lengthened. 9-10.62 carried out escape trials from a depth of 260 feet off Malta. 9.11.63 arrived at Gosport to join the 1st Submarine Squadron. 13.7.65 damaged in collision with HMS YARMOUTH. 29.8.69 paid off at Portsmouth for disposal. 1972 sold to H G Pounds of Portsmouth and laid up. 1979 brought into scrapyard and breaking up commenced.

HMS TOTEM (May 53)

'T' class submarine built in Devonport Dockyard launched 28.9.43 and completed 9.1.45 for service with the British Pacific Fleet. 10.46 paid off for refit during which Snort was added. 1947 2nd Submarine Flotilla, Home Fleet. 1952-53 rebuilt and lengthened. 15.6.53 Coronation Review at Spithead. 1958-59 refitted at Chatham. 25.1.63 arrived Portsmouth after two years in the Mediterranean. 28.1.63 recommissioned for 1st Submarine Squadron. 16.6.65 returned to Gosport for the last time as a Royal Navy vessel. Sold to Israel. 10.11.67 commissioned as DAKAR after refit at Portsmouth. 25.1.68 Lost, with all hands, Eastern Mediterranean on delivery voyage.

HMS TRAFALGAR (June 53)

Battle class destroyer built by Swan Hunter on the Tyne. Launched 12.1.44 and completed 23.7.45 and joined 19th Destroyer Flotilla in the Pacific. 1947 reduced to Reserve and not recommissioned again until 1958 but did go to sea on occasions as the mobile headquarters of the Admiral Commanding Reserve Ships. 15.6.53 Coronation Review at Spithead. 20.5.58 recommissioned at Portsmouth for service as leader of the 7th Destroyer Squadron in the Home/Mediterranean Fleet. 5.63 paid off into Reserve at Portsmouth. 7.70 broken up at Dalmuir.

HMS TRIUMPH (July 52)

Light fleet aircraft carrier built by Hawthorn, Leslie on the Tyne launched 2.10.44 and completed 9.4.46. Flagship of Flag Officer (Air) in the Mediterranean Fleet followed by some service in Home Waters before converting (4.53) to Cadet Training Ship. 10.55 visited Leningrad. Paid off early 1956. 12.57 conversion to Heavy Repair Ship began at Portsmouth; suspended early 1960. Restarted mid-1962; 9.10.64 carried out preliminary sea trials. 7.1.65 commissioned at Portsmouth. 1965-72 based at Singapore then paid off into Reserve at Chatham. 9.12.81 left Chatham to be broken up in Spain.

HMS TRUMP (October 59)

'T' class submarine built by Vickers Armstrongs at Barrow launched 25.3.44 and completed 9.7.44 for the Eastern Fleet and the Pacific. 1946 snort fitted. 1949 1st Submarine Flotilla. 1955-56 reconstructed and lengthened by 20 feet. 1961 in 4th Submarine Squadron, Australian waters, until 1969 with refits at Sydney 1962 and 1965. 10.1.69 left Sydney for the UK—the last RN submarine to be based in Australia. 8.71 arrived Newport to be broken up.

HMS TRUNCHEON (September 51)

'T' class submarine built by Devonport Dockyard launched 22.2.44 and completed 25.5.45. Served in Home Waters. 1949-50 refitted with experimental equipment on starboard side of forward casing (see photo). 1952-53 reconstructed and lengthened. 15.1.62 at Rosyth for refit and re-engining. 7.1.63 recommissioned. 1965 refitted at Chatham. 1966 sold to Israel. 9.1.68 commissioned into Israeli Navy at Portsmouth and renamed DOLPHIN. Deleted 1977.

HMS TUDOR (February 53)

Later 'T' class submarine built at Devonport Dockyard, launched 23.9.42 and completed 16.1.44. Operated during the last year of the war in the Far East, based at Trincomalee and Fremantle. Post war served principally in Home Waters until 1954 and then spent some time East of Suez, carrying out exercises in the Indian Ocean 8.54 and 6.58. 1959 refitted at Rosyth for further Home Service. Sold at Chatham 1.7.63 and towed to Faslane later in the month to be broken up.

HMS TYNE (May 55)

Destroyer depot ship built by Scotts at Greenock launched 28.2.40 and completed 28.2.41. Served with the Home Fleet until 1944 and then transferred to the Pacific. 1947 Reserve at Harwich. 1949 refitted at Devonport. 1950 Reserve Fleet depot ship at Malta. 1952 Flagship of Flag Officer, Second-in-Command, Far East in Japanese waters during Korean War. 14.5.54 arrived Devonport and then became Flagship of C-in-C, Home Fleet. 1957-58 refit at Portsmouth. 1961 relinquished flag for the last time and became accommodation ship at Portsmouth then Devonport. 1968 Maintenance ship for Reserve Fleet at Devonport. 9.72 broken up at Barrow.

HMS TYRIAN (June 53)

Troubridge class destroyer built by Swan Hunter on the Tyne. Launched 27.7.42 and completed 8.4.43 for the 24th Destroyer Flotilla in the Mediterranean. 9.9.43 Salerno. 15.8.44 South France landing. 1945 Pacific Fleet. 9.45 occupation of Shanghai. 1946 Reserve. 10.6.51 arrived at Liverpool to convert to Type 16 frigate. 8.52 joined 2nd Training Squadron at Portland. 11.56 reduced to Reserve at Chatham. 1957 transferred to Lisahally. 9.3.65 arrived at Troon to be broken up.

TRV 4 (September 51)

Torpedo recovery vessel built by Rowhedge Ironworks and launched 20.2.43. In October 1949 was offered by the Admiralty for commercial charter but was not taken up. Photo shows vessel with a torpedo on chocks on deck. Ultimate fate unknown but still in service as late as 1969.

HMS ULSTER (July 50)

Destroyer built by Swan Hunter on the Tyne launched 9.11.42 and completed 30.6.43. 23.11.43 in action with German torpedo boats in the Channel. 6.6.44 part of the covering forces for Operation Neptune. Transferred to Pacific Fleet and (1.4.45) damaged by Kamikaze and towed to Leyte by HMS GAMBIA. Repairs at Chatham completed 2.46. 1946-50 Training ship at Rosyth. 1950 Dartmouth Flotilla. 1954 at Chatham converting to Type 15 frigate. 7.3.57 8th Frigate Squadron on Home/West Indies service. 1964-65 refitted at Devonport then joined 2nd Frigate Squadron. 1967 attached to HMS DRYAD as navigation training ship. 1971 Devonport harbour training ship for HMS RALEIGH. 11.80 arrived at Inverkeithing to be broken up.

HMS ULYSSES (April 51)

Destroyer built by Cammell Laird at Birkenhead launched 22.4.43 and completed 23.12.43. Joined 3rd Destroyer Flotilla. 1944 escorted convoys to Russia and covered D-Day landings. 1.45 transferred to the Pacific Fleet with the 25th Destroyer Flotilla. 1946 Devonport Reserve. 1951 Plymouth Local Flotilla. 1954 being converted to Type 15 frigate at Devonport. 2.1.55 6th Frigate Squadron on Home/Mediterranean general service commission. 4.58 present at the Christmas Island nuclear tests. 5.9.58 returned to Devonport after a round the world voyage. Late 1960 in Reserve at Devonport and Portsmouth until 1971. 2.2.71 arrived at Faslane to be broken up.

HMS UNTIRING (1955)

Built by Vickers Armstongs on the Tyne launched 20.1.43 and completed 9.6.43. Operated in the Mediterranean sinking a number of vessels including the German submarine chasers UJ 6075 (27.4.44) and UJ 6078 (10.6.44), both off Toulon. 1945 loaned to Greece and renamed XIFIAS. 1952 returned to the Royal Navy at Malta. 6.52 sailed to the UK but suffered engine trouble and had to be towed from Cape St Vincent to Portsmouth by the tug EARNER, arriving 30.6.52. 1952-55 in Home waters. 1956 laid up. 25.7.57 expended as an Asdic target off Start Point.

HMS VANGUARD (May 52)

Battleship built by John Brown & Co Ltd on Clydebank. Launched 30.11.44 and completed 25.4.46. The last and largest British battleship. Carried HM King George VI on a tour to South Africa in early 1947; a tour planned for 1948 was cancelled. 1948 to 10.54 carried out fleet and training duties interspersed with various exercises. 9.53 during Exercise 'Mariner' she proved herself to be a better seaboat and more stable gun platform in adverse weather conditions than the American battleship IOWA. In Reserve from 10.54 at Portsmouth until being sold for breaking up at Faslane in 1960.

HMS VENGEANCE (July 51)

Light Fleet Carrier built by Swan Hunters on the Tyne launched 23.2.44 and completed 15.1.45. At Sydney on VJ Day and performed repatriation duties before seeing service as a training carrier. 1950-51 was Flagship of the Third Aircraft Carrier Squadron. 1952-55 operated by the Royal Australian Navy. 1955-56 in Reserve 14.12.56 sold to Brazil. 1957-60 Reconstructed at Rotterdam. 13.1.61 Sailed from Rotterdam under her new name MINAS GERAIS. 1976-81 Refitted to give a further 10 year's active service.

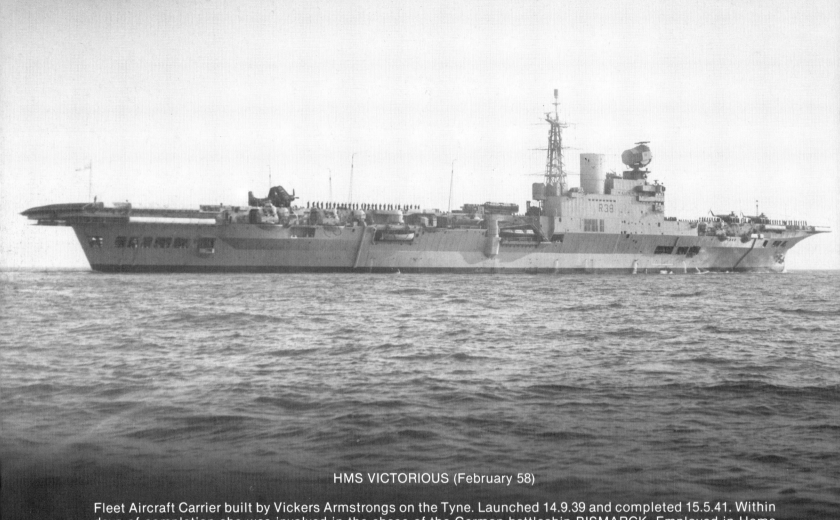

HMS VICTORIOUS (February 58)

Fleet Aircraft Carrier built by Vickers Armstrongs on the Tyne. Launched 14.9.39 and completed 15.5.41. Within days of completion she was involved in the chase of the German battleship BISMARCK. Employed in Home Waters until mid-1944 with detached duty for the 'Pedestal' convoy to Malta 8.42 and Operation Torch 11.42. 1944-45 Eastern & Pacific Fleets. 9.5.45 damaged by Kamikaze aircraft. 10.45 returned to Portsmouth. March 1950 entered Portsmouth Dockyard for almost total reconstruction which was completed in 1958. 1962-3 refitted. 11.67 damaged by fire and paid off. 7.70 arrived at Faslane to be broken up.

HMS VIDAL (November 57)

Survey vessel built at Chatham Dockyard and launched 31.7.51 and completed 29.3.54. Operated in Home Waters before moving to the West Indies. 12.54 returned to Chatham. The next eleven years were spent surveying in Home and West Indies waters with regular refits at Chatham. From 1966 her surveying duties were in the Far East until 1970 when she paid off for disposal. 6.76 Broken up at Bruges.

HMS VIGILANT (June 57)

Destroyer built by Swan Hunter on the Tyne launched 22.12.42 and completed 10.9.43. 1944 Arctic convoys and D-Day operations before joining the 26th Destroyer Flotilla in the East Indies early in 1945. 16.5.45 destruction of the Japanese heavy cruiser HAGURO in the Malacca Straits. 1946 Mediterranean. 1949 Reserve at Portsmouth. 1951-52 converted to Type 15 frigate. 1953 6th Frigate Squadron, Home Fleet. 27.10.54 in collision with HMS RELENTLESS in the Minches. 1956 joined Dartmouth Training Squadron after refit. 1963 reduced to Reserve at Devonport. 4.6.65 arrived at Faslane to be broken up.

HMS VIGO (June 57)

Battle class destroyer built by Fairfield at Govan, launched 27.9.45 and completed 9.12.46. Placed in Reserve on completion. 7.49 joined 3rd Destroyer Flotilla in the Mediterranean. 1954 replaced FINISTERRE as seagoing gunnery training and firing ship based at Portsmouth. 8.59 reduced to Reserve at Portsmouth. 27.11.64 towed from Portsmouth to Faslane to be broken up.

HMS VOLAGE (August 55)

Destroyer built by Whites at Cowes launched 15.12.43 and completed 26.5.44. Home Fleet on Arctic convoy and Norway strike duty then joined 26th Destroyer Flotilla in Indian Ocean early in 1945. 1946 3rd Destroyer Flotilla in Mediterranean. 22.10.46 bows blown off by mine in Corfu Channel. Repaired at Malta. 17.5.49 arrived Portsmouth to pay off into Reserve. 1952 conversion to Type 15 frigate at Cowes. 1954 3rd Training Squadron based on Londonderry. 1956 Reserve, first at Portsmouth then Rosyth where she refitted before becoming harbour training ship at Portsmouth in 1964. 1972 sold to H G Pounds at Portsmouth for breaking up, in whose yard part of the hull can still (1985) be seen.

HMS WHITESAND BAY (August 54)

Frigate built by Harland & Wolff at Belfast launched 16.12.44 and completed 30.7.45. After trials joined Pacific Fleet until 3.47 when she transferred to the Mediterranean. 9.48 joined the America & West Indies Station. 19.7.49 left Bermuda for Hong Kong and joined the 4th Frigate Flotilla. 1950-52 took an active part in the Korean War. 24.8.54 arrived at Portsmouth to pay off having covered 223,000 miles since 10.45. 13.2.56 arrived Charlestown to be broken up; the first of the 'Bay' class to suffer that fate.

HMS WIAY (May 52)

Isles class trawler built by Cook, Welton & Gemmell at Beverley launched 26.4.44 and completed as a danlayer. 4.53 listed as Category I Reserve. 15.6.53 Coronation Review at Spithead representing the Reserve Fleet. 10.56 listed as Operational Reserve. Sold 15.12.60 or 10.61 (sources vary) and renamed ENRICO CARLO, sailing under the Honduran flag.

HMS WIZARD (July 51)

Destroyer built by Vickers Armstrongs at Barrow launched 29.9.43 and completed 30.3.44. Early service in the Home Fleet was followed by service in the Pacific Fleet from 1.45. 1946 Plymouth Local Flotilla. 3.50 2nd Training Flotilla. 1953 conversion to Type 15 frigate at Devonport. 2.11.54 recommissioned for 5th Frigate Squadron on Home and Mediterranean service. 16.5.57 returned to Chatham for refit and Reserve. 1962 8th Frigate Squadron West Indies. 1964 Dartmouth Training Squadron. 1966 paid off for disposal. 7.3.67 arrived at Inverkeithing to be broken up.

HMS WOODBRIDGE HAVEN (June 53)

Built by Swan Hunters on the Tyne launched as "Loch Torridon" 13.1.45. Completed as WOODBRIDGE HAVEN, a submarine depot and target ship, and operated as such with the 3rd Submarine Flotilla until 1954. Converted at Chatham to headquarters ship for coastal minesweepers and commissioned 9.9.55 for service in the Mediterranean and Far East. 11.7.63 arrived Portsmouth to pay off. 1965 de-equipped and left Portsmouth 9.8.65 in tow of tug SAMSONIA to be broken up at Blyth.

HMS WRANGLER (June 53)

Wager class destroyer built by Vickers Armstrongs at Barrow launched 30.12.43 and completed 14.7.44 for Home Fleet service. 1.45 transferred to British Pacific Fleet. 1946 Rosyth Local Flotilla. 1950 Boys' training ship. 5.51 commenced conversion to Type 15 frigate at Liverpool. 31.3.53 sailed from the Mersey for work-up. 9.53 5th Frigate Squadron Mediterranean. 5.2.55 dragged anchors in gale and ran aground near Nice. 7.2.55 refloated. 1956 refitted. 21.11.56 transferred to South Africa at Cardiff and renamed VRYSTAAT. 4.76 sunk as a target by frigate PRESIDENT STEYN.

HMS ZAMBESI (June 51)

Destroyer built by Cammell Laird at Birkenhead. Launched 21.11.43 and completed 15.7.44. 1944 2nd Destroyer
Flotilla. 1945 4th Destroyer Flotilla. 1946 Reserve at Devonport. 1950 target ship for the 3rd Submarine Flotilla
based on Rothesay. 9.51 visited Baltic Ports with the Flotilla. 1953 refitted at Penarth. 1954 Reserve at Cardiff.
12.2.59 arrived Briton Ferry to be broken up.

HMS ZEST (June 53)

Destroyer built by Thornycroft, Southampton launched 14.10.43 and completed 20.7.44. Served in Home Waters to the end of the war. 1946 4th Destroyer Flotilla Home Fleet. 1947 Torpedo training ship at Portsmouth and Portland. 1949 2nd Training Flotilla. 1952 reduced to Reserve at Chatham. 2.54 began conversion to Type 15 frigate. 1956 3rd Training Squadron based on Londonderry. 1958 4th Frigate Squadron. 1961 extended refit at Malta. 26.8.64 sailed from Portsmouth to join 24th Escort Squadron in Far East. 4.7.68 returned to Devonport to pay off into Reserve. 8.70 arrived Dalmuir to be broken up.

INDEX